Smile
And
Be Free

KEVIN PEDRAZA

To order additional copies of this book, contact:
Xlibris
844-714-8691
www.Xlibris.com
Orders@Xlibris.com

ISBN: Softcover   978-1-6641-4233-6
        Hardcover   978-1-6641-4234-3
        EBook   978-1-6641-4232-9

Library of Congress Control Number: 2020922524

Print information available on the last page

Rev. date: 11/20/2020

Why be sad when hope is right around the corner?

I would like to dedicate this book to God for giving me the opportunity
to accomplish things I never thought I could.

Jeremiah 29:11

Contents

Dear Reader,

Your imagination is about to run wild. Each page will come to life in its own unique way. Embrace the journey with every twist and turn along the way. Break free and let your emotions guide you through each passage. Do not forget to smile, for it will be an epic ending.

Love

How can I explain something that is even beyond my own understanding? It is something that is crazy, yet it has its moments when it is just amazing. Some of us use it like it means something, while others use it like a habit. It could even be your best friend or the one thing you wish having. But it can also leave you miserable, not knowing how to hold on. For some of us, we want to show it, yet we were never taught how to. And for others, they hope for it as though it hasn't found them. Yet most of us abuse it, and for some reason we still pursue it. It's a privilege to have it, but we pretend like it is useless. Some would even die for it, while others ask themselves if it could even be real. But if you want to know the outcome of it all, it will all depend on how you use this thing called…

Beauty Within

If my sense of touch was to lose all meaning. And my eyes could no longer see clearly. The beauty of life would still remain, for it is something that can only be felt within the heart.

A Place So Mysterious

I didn't realize how much our love would grow. That the attraction that first brought us together would reach beyond passion. That our relationship would lead us to a place so mysterious and beyond belief. It would be like...

Can I Be Honest

I'm such a mess. My heart loves to hide because the truth is harder than a lie. The dark just seems safer than the light. I keep pretending like healing is farther than by my side. All I have to do is lay my secrets at the cross, for freedom is found when I am honest.

Proverbs 24:26

Against All Odds

I wish I could just make you turn around, so you could see these tears running down my face. It may have been easy for you to pretend, but for me you were the only one. We shared the laughter and the pain, yet there's nothing left but an empty space. Against all odds I know I will be okay. Your memories will soon fade away as I sit here and watch you walk away.

Can't Compare

Stand up tall even when your back is against a wall. Hold your head up high because you're a star in the night sky. You're that little bit of hope that we're all searching for. You seem to be that helping hand when nobody else is around. And just when you're about to walk away, turn around. For no one will ever be compared to you.

Completely

When the stars are shining, I miss looking up at them with you by my side. When the sun rises and sets in the horizon, I miss holding you while we sit in the sand. And when the rain falls from up above, my heart aches knowing I completely miss you.

Te Amo

Desde el primer momento en que te vi. No te pude decir, porque no era tan fácil como me imaginaba. Otra oportunidad a lo mejor nunca la voy a tener. Antes de que te vayas, no se si nos volveremos a ver. Espero que con mis palabras, puedas saber todo lo que siento por ti.

Beauty

I thought I knew what beauty was, but just like always I was wrong. You caught me by surprise and now my life will never be the same. Not sure how to tell you, but every time you come around you take my breath away. I'm nervous to even look into your eyes, yet I can't walk away. True beauty will no longer be hard to find. It will never be far away. For beauty like you is all I need.

A Love Letter

If my voice was gone forever, I would by no means stop loving you. For a love letter would be waiting for you every time you open your eyes.

Can't Tell You

I thought I said all I needed to say. How can I be so far away from the truth. I can't even look into your eyes because of what I am still holding inside. I don't know what to do, but I have to figure something out before I complicate things even more. I can't take back what has already been done, so why can't I just be man enough and tell you.

Dreams Do Come True

You already know that I am no Casanova. But if I had to move heaven and earth just to put a smile on your face, without a doubt I would. Late at night you close your eyes and dream of a love that is everlasting. Well, open your eyes because dreams do come true.

Bailando Contigo

Coloca tus manos arriba y no te preocupes, porque aquí estoy a tu lado. Da una vuelta, porque te ves bien linda. Como mueves la cintura, sin mi ayuda. Así es como epmieza, ahora mueve la cabeza y no pierdas el ritmo. Da otra vuelta porque el tiempo no importa. Bailando contigo es lo major del mundo.

Among The Stars

The day I have to let you go, it will only be because it's time to place you among the stars.

Fatty

You were never a mistake, but instead a blessing. Life is a gift, which is why every moment I spend with you is worth living it to the fullest. To all those around us you are simply my sister. Yet I see someone that at my lowest, you were there to lift me up. At my happiest, you were there to celebrate with me. At my darkest, you were the light to lead the way. And at my saddest, you wiped away my tears. You will forever be more than just my sister. To me, you are my heart. Which is the second most valuable part of me. God will always have my soul, for it is Him who I give all the glory to. Yet His love is felt when I am with you. Love you forever.

Kasey Pedraza

For Me To Find

I was given two hands, so I could hold you and never let you go. Two legs, so I could run to you and never look back. Two eyes, so I could see your beauty and perfection. Yet only one heart because the other one was given to you for me to find.

Give, For I Am With You

Give the heavens a reason to smile. Give life a fighting chance, even when all the odds are against you. You were made to shine beyond all the sorrows you hold inside. True love will never leave you empty handed. And when you feel like you are all alone, don't worry. For I will be with you.

Galatians 2:20

Hardest Thing Ever

How do I walk away without hurting you? I wish I could lie, but I can't keep pretending like everything is alright. I made up my mind, even though I know you're going to cry. All I ask, is for you not to ask me why. Because this will always be the hardest thing I have ever done in my life.

Hearts Will Know Me

Let me be the change for someone who has nothing. For then, and only then, will I know my life was meant for something. The world may never know my name, but that is okay, because my goal was to touch hearts and let them know who I am.

How Far

How far is the east from the west? I feel like I am on an endless road. I yearn for my darkness to turn into light. Each day is like I am at war or just one mistake away. I just don't want to end up where you found me. I can't bear to be the man I have been. Here, I am wondering how far I must go, but my arms just don't seem to reach from one side to the other.

I Did It All For You

It has been a long day, but I do it all to see that smile on your face. Every day I wake up with you on my mind, hoping I will make it through the day. I still remember when we first met, a bond that only you and I understood. We did so much in a short period of time, but who knew it would all come to an end. Pain is real because ever since you left, that is all that I feel. There is so much I want to tell you, but I know I will when I see you again.

Heaven

If death was just a memory and life was a blink of an eye away, could there be such a place where hope is breathtaking. Where my worries would no longer be because I would be free.

Philippians 3:20

I Love You More

I loved you yesterday, I love you today, and tomorrow I will simply say; "I love you more! More than what you can imagine or even start to wonder. I love you."

Destiny

I can see you're sad, even when you try to hide it. No need to deny it, no need to fight it. It may take you some time, but don't you cry. I know deep inside you can make it through this. Don't be scared, I am still right there. Even if you can't see me, I am still with you in your prayers. I know we didn't plan this, but that's what destiny is.

Different Intentions

You used to be someone I denied, someone I used to hide. I couldn't even stand having you by my side. And when you decided to walk away, I was glad you went away. Now when I think about it over and over again, I should have given you the respect that you deserved. I Should have kept it real instead of telling you all the things that made you feel so good. I know there is nothing I can do, but my intentions are not the same as then. I just hope that with time I can show you how much I actually miss you.

My Prayer

God fill me with that joy I can't explain. Can I also get that peace that will ease my pain. How about wisdom, to know when to stay or simply walk away. But most of all, can I get that love that will never change. All this, I pray.

Could This Be Real

In a world where everything is meant to be broken. Where hope is sometimes hard to find. Even when I try to hide, my tears keep pulling me back to all the pain I have inside. I want to close my eyes and call it a night. Yet, as I stare into the sky, I start to realize this is nothing more than a…

Life Without You

Sometimes I wonder if our greatest disappointments are a reminder of how much we need you. If it takes a thousand tears and a broken heart to know you are near, then let your will be done instead of mine. I know I've doubted you my whole life as if your love wasn't enough. So many sleepless nights; yet, I finally understand that life without you is a waste of time.

Imagine

When that day comes, I can only imagine. Will I be able to look you in the eyes or will your presence be overwhelming? Will I be able to speak at all or will you just take my breath away? What will it be like when I finally get the chance to meet you? I may never know, yet my heart can't wait to forever be with you.

Hebrews 11:1

In Your Arms

Being wrapped in your arms is exactly where I belonged. As you played with my hair, I couldn't help it but smile. I knew as I closed my eyes, you would never let me go. As my heart came to an end, I knew it would be okay. Because comfort only came when I would be in your arms.

It's Undeniable

It's so incredible how things work themselves out. Unbelievable. Like a dream come true. If time couldn't hold us apart, then it's undeniable that we were meant to be. I think it's plain to see that you're the only one for me. Lets just say it's undesirable for us to be away from one another.

Espero Verte Aquí

Por qué estás tan triste por mí? Yo estoy en un lugar lleno de luz. Es tan bello aquí, que al fin puedo descansar. Si pudiera devolver el tiempo, te diría, no llores por mí. Porque cuando te toque, espero verte aquí.

I Might Be Near

You get frustrated when I am nowhere to be found. I know you hate it when I am not around, but I need you not to frown. Don't be afraid, I promise I won't disappear. Instead, let me make things clear, and tell you how I truly feel. You mean more to me than what you'll ever know. So before you let out a tear, look around because I might be near.

Here We Go Again

Sometimes the wrong just feels so right. I can't tell you what it is, but let me tell you what it feels like. Here we go again; you drive me insane. The more I love you, the more I suffer. We tried to go our separate ways, yet that was so yesterday because today we are running right back. I know we said things and did things that we didn't mean. Maybe it was all me, maybe our relationship isn't as crazy as it seems. Here we go again.

Face The Facts

I must have been out of my mind to think you were the one for me. I can't believe I wanted you so bad, but now looking back I'm glad I'm done with all that. It's time to face the facts because the person I am now, doesn't want you back.

Just Need A Reason

Give me a reason, just enough to try again. I know we are not perfect, as a matter of fact, we always disagree. We always speak our minds without thinking twice. As hurt as we might be, we just need a fresh new start. So instead of packing your bags, give me just one good reason to ask you not to go away.

Looking For A Purpose

I still have my doubts, but I think that part you have already figured out. I'm an open book, yet I can't seem to be able to turn the page. Maybe tomorrow will bring comfort because I am falling apart. I'm barely breathing, like a broken heart that is still beating. This whole time I've been looking for a purpose instead of just starting my life.

What God Has Done For Me

You break my chains and make me free. You take all my pain and give me peace. How can it be when I didn't even believe. You heard my cry and didn't push me to the side. You opened my eyes and helped me realize what was right. I no longer ask myself why because I know I was living a lie. You gave me hope when I thought I was running out of time.

Just In Luck

If you ever wondered where the healing begins, well then, you are just in luck because this is where it all starts. All you have to do is let your walls fall to the ground. Don't be ashamed to look up because this is where you belong. It is time to face all of your fears and let your light shine. This is the moment that was made just for you. So don't wait because healing only comes to those who believe.

Dare You

Dare you to move. Dare you to smile, for you are beautiful. Dare you to wipe away your sorrows, for hope is right around the corner. I dare you to move. Dare you to lift your head, for you're on top of the world. Go ahead, smile, believe, and laugh with joy. I dare you to. No more shame, tears, or pain. Let your light shine and dare to live. For we can only go as far as we dare to see. Dare… Dare to be free.

If Life Could Speak

If your life could speak beyond your wildest dreams, would it be worth making it a reality? Would it be like an untold story, and each step of the way would be so breath taking? Life has a purpose and a meaning behind every day. The only question there really is and probably ever will be is…?

Want A New Life

Didn't think I was worth a thing. Life was hard, yet I didn't have a choice. Running was all I knew. My life was a mystery, and I knew I had to change before I became history. God you created me to glorify you, but the way I've been living I deserve to go to hell. I may have made a mess of my life, but I know it's not too late. God, wait for me. I want a new life with you.

My Greatest Fight

I just need some time because I am still haunted by all the memories. I am still breaking while you are falling asleep. Underneath it all, I still feel captive from all the pain I had to endure. It's not easy to lift myself up when I am drowning in my sorrows. Yet I am ready to forgive, but forgetting is the hardest fight I ever had to face.

A Tear

If I were a tear in your eye…I would roll down your cheek to let you know I stand by your side, and end up on your lips to let you know it's going to be okay.

Kissing You

If I could give you a kiss, would it be slow and tender. Or could it be breathtaking to the point we are both left with wanting more. For if a kiss could be so magical, would it be worth the wait. Is it true, that the force we feel would entice us to not stop. What kind of kiss would it be once our lips were to…

My New Beginning

They say you are crazy and that I am out of my mind. I want to be right, but the choice I make will impact the rest of my life. But if falling in love with you is so wrong, can life ever be the same without you? Even if it is just you and I, life would have no end. Because every time I look at you, all I see is a new beginning.

My Heart Is In Your Hands

If I could tell you everything I feel for you I wouldn't say a word. All I would need to do is place my heart in your hands. For it is no longer a matter of words, but instead of the heart.

No More Pain

Don't have much time, yet I'm glad you're here next to me. Tonight may be the last time I get to be with you. But don't you worry, for when you think of me, that just means I am thinking of you too. Life was good, thanks to you. When things got hard you were there for me. Never once did you leave my side, always trying to take care of me. You must have been sent from up above just for me. This, I believe is true, for nothing in this world can compare to you. This cancer had me beat, but because of you, I fought for one more day. Yet the time has come for me to let you go. But before I do, I just want you to know that I am grateful I fell in love with you.

Never

It has never been about how long we go without seeing each other that makes me miss you. But instead, the simple fact of knowing I may never find anyone else like you.

Only When

You only start to miss someone when you let them go. You only feel like giving up when you're no longer strong. You only realize what you had, when it is nowhere to be found. You only know how far you can go, when you don't stop believing.

No Puedo Seguir Sufriendo

Mi alma desfallece, a tal grado que no puede recuperarse. No me pidas que te perdone, porque no sé si tenga fuerzas para eso. Cansado estoy, que no sirvo para amarte. Es muy tarde para que te arrepientas. Ya no tengo aliento para odiarte, ni tampoco pienso seguir sufriendo. Sé que va a ser muy difícil olvidarte, pero como tú me lo enseñaste, por fin, el tiempo llegó para dejarte.

Off My Chest

How do I tell the person I used to love, that they can't have my heart anymore? I gave you my soul, yet that wasn't good enough for you. I used to cry myself to sleep hoping there would be no more lies. You took my love for granted and now I have no more tears to cry. Brokenhearted, because I truly loved you. You had me once, but now I am on my own. Sorry if you thought I was waiting on you. All I needed was to get this off my chest.

Go Back

You said sorry, hoping I would turn around. You came running with tears in your eyes, but I had already made up my mind. Please don't waste my time and instead go back to the one you thought would never leave your side. I might say hi whenever I pass you by, but don't get excited because I would never want you to be mine.

I Need You The Most

Dear Father,

I am praying to you about a friend. Which concerns me the most, yet I don't know what else I can do. He says he's trying, but I am scared for him because he is always crying. He feels like he's losing his mind, even though he has a wife who is always praying for him. Lord if he won't talk to you, then hear it from me. I am determined to pray for him daily. Jesus just have your way with him because I am not willing to give up on him. I know he isn't the best of men, but deep inside he knows he needs you the most. God I know this is hurting you, but the person I've been praying for is really me.

Couldn't Break Me

You tried to keep me all the way down, but it's funny how I never hit the ground. I got no time to frown because my smile doesn't look so good when it's upside down. If you ever see me around, just know I've come a long way from when you tried to break me down.

Overcome

I cannot stop staring into the night sky, looking for a ray of hope. I have so much on my mind; nothing seems to be going right. Yet I can't let all this get the best of me. I've been here before, but this time I am not alone. The great *I AM* is holding me. There is nothing I cannot overcome, when God is in control of my life.

When God made me, He made sure I came out with a smile

Ready to face an unknown world with a known God

Thank you God for everything

Something New

We sometimes lose things to keep us going strong. But today is a whole new day and I don't have time to talk about the past. Instead, let me break free from the person I used to be. I don't want to play it safe because fear will never keep me from happiness. So tired of running away just because I feel like this is all I can take. I may have made mistakes, but my dreams will keep me from losing hope.

Still A Reason To Believe

Maybe some things happen only to bring us a better future. I know right now it may be hard to see, but the pain that you're feeling can't compare to the joy that is coming. So hold on because there is still a reason for you to believe. All these things will soon fade away even if it may take a little time. Someday, somehow, all this will make sense.

Missing Piece

A million broken pieces. I have never seen so many. Maybe one of these would be the perfect fit. So much in common, yet I can't find the one for me. I just need one last piece and my heart will be complete. Emptiness is no longer my concern, but instead the reason why I need to take a chance. A chance to find my missing piece.

Slipping Away

I have been praying and hoping things between us would get better. You have every right to leave because of the way I have been acting lately. Let's just say I have a lot of apologizing to do. We seem to argue every other day and every time we do; I see you slipping away. I know it might not be easy, but I am not willing to let you go without a fight.

Soon

I used to be someone that could make you laugh. Someone that would do anything just to see you smile. Now I am just someone in an old photograph. And soon I will just be a memory from the past.

Lost A Part Of Me

I should have held on tighter instead of lying to myself. I didn't mean a single word, but I was foolish enough to let you go. As much as I try to keep it together, deep down I know I am just falling apart. As much as I need you back in my life, I just can't let go of my pride. Things will never be the same because a part of me is lost forever.

Memory Lane

Take me to that familiar place. All the way back to memory lane, so I can show you all that we had. I just want to remind you that you will never perish. The future has never looked so bright because love always shines. In case you forgot, that is how I will find you.

Thinking Of You

I don't know why, but you are the only one on my mind. It's like I just have to be next to you. You already know, when we are together it's all about you. As long as we are spending time, I know everything is going to be alright. I never worry because I know that even when we are far apart, you are the only one worth fighting for.

The One Place I Want To Be

Every time I try to hold your hand, I just melt right between your fingertips. It's amazing how you always take my breath away. I just can't hesitate anymore, so let me hold you tight because I have never done this before. Let me look into your heart because that is the only place I want to see myself in. If I am there, then I know we were meant to be.

The Note

If you were to ask me what life would be like if we were together, I would say, "Take my hand because words just wouldn't be enough to let you know." I would tell you to close your eyes and imagine every place you ever wanted to go. Then imagine every single thing you ever wanted to do. And before you opened your eyes, I would leave a note in your hands as I would take a step into the unknown. The note would say…

Not The Same

If I were to fall asleep without thinking of you, then it would be a night I wouldn't want to remember.

Take A Chance On Me

Every time you try, you always end up getting crushed. Now you wonder if you did something wrong. Yet when I try to turn that frown upside down, you think I am just the same. I know you may be scared, but I can help you make it clear. If you want someone you can trust and that will never give up, who can love you no matter what, then just take a chance. Just take a chance on me.

Love Me More Than Air

Could you still love me the same when I am no more? As thoughts of me fill your memory? Could you embrace all we ever had, like how the sea hugs the shore? For if I were to fade away, like the air you breathe. Would you let me go or hold on to me?

You Calmed The Sea

Your plans are always higher than mine. Yet there are days I don't have a clue what it is you want me to do. Like when the waves were about to take me under, I prayed for you to part the waters. I held my breath and did everything I could to stay above the waves. But I knew that on my own I would eventually drown. I cried out to you like never before and put all my trust in you. When I least expected it, you calmed the sea and gave me the strength to walk on water.

Take Over Me

Sometimes I wonder if our greatest disappointments are only a reminder of how much we need you. If it takes a thousand tears and a broken heart just to know you are near, then let your will be done instead of mine. I know I've doubted you my whole life, as if your love wasn't enough. So many sleepless nights, yet I finally understand that life without you is a waste of time.

What I Never Had

Don't cry, everything is going to be alright. Come here, and let me wipe away those tears. No more worries, I am here to hold you through the night. I didn't plan for things to be this way, but I guess everything happens for a reason. I am trying to give you the life I never had, yet the more I try, I just seem to be losing my mind. But I promise you, that we will make it through this. So now close your eyes, because maybe by the time you wake up, I can give you the world.

What Life Could have been

So many questions running through my mind. It almost seems like it was just yesterday we were having the time of our lives. Now all I have are the tears that run down my face. I should have held your hand and told you how much you meant to me. I should have picked you up like if we were free from all the pain and suffering of this world. I should have kissed you longer to remind you of the love I have for you. If I could have told you anything, it is that I was scared of losing you. For life without you is no life at all.

Will I Know

You say our love is strong, yet I feel weak. How will I know if this is really love or just a moment worth holding on to? How can you be so sure, while I have no clue on what to do? Tell me, how will I know?

Crushed

I still remember when we first met. You had tears running down your face. I didn't want to ask. You said it was because of your ex. All I could say was maybe it's time for a change. I wasn't talking about us, just simply that you needed a man that you can trust. I know its been a while since we last talked, but you decided to go back and try it again. Now you're back, with your heart crushed.

You Are Worth More

Anyone can give you all the things in the world, but to the right person you will be worth more than anything this world can offer.

You Mean The World To Me

You have a smile that just takes all the pain away. You make the best of everything despite all that you been through. You give me hope, to the point that I just want to give life another try. When you and I laugh, it's just the beauty of what you hold inside. When you go, I promise I will try not to cry and instead remember what you told me. Believe, for I am not far, but in your heart.

You Never Let Me Fall

You build me up and give me strength to carry on. Never do you let me fall; you instead give me words that bring me hope. Late at night when comfort seems so far away, I know I can count on you to take all my worries away. Because of you, life will never be the same.

Young Love

Just between you and me, we have a serious bond. I might drive you crazy, yet we never stop having fun. My reputation almost made you change your mind. But I believe you're the one, even though our love is still young.

Where I Belong

If I can make you smile, then I know this is where I belong. I know this may seem like a dream, yet I dare you to open your eyes, for I am right here next to you. Come close and I promise to never let you go. It's not always going to be easy, but I believe our love is strong. Lets not worry, for today is not about tears or pain. Instead lets hold hands and make it last.

When Nothing Else

I don't know what I did to deserve someone as amazing as you. It's like all my dreams and hopes became a reality the moment I laid eyes on you. Everything around me can't compare to you because life without you, is just unimaginable. When nothing else will do, then I hope my words will remind you of how I feel for you.

Such A Journey

If I must go on such a journey just to know that you are okay, then it will be a journey worth traveling.

To Be Desired

I may not always have the brightest days. And at times, my nights seem too long. I have one too many insecurities, which come with a lot of attention. I long for passion, but what I truly wish for is to be desired.

We

We get all excited when we see each other. It feels as though it was the first time we ever met. It has been said that nothing good lasts forever, yet the question everybody asks, is how do we make it last? We just keep things fresh every single day. We talk on the phone for hours and write letters to each other every other day. We go through problems just like everybody else, yet nothing is going to break us apart. As long as we stick together, we will somehow find the strength to carry on. We may not know everything about each other, but without a doubt we are each other's better half.

Thanks To You

When I needed you the most you were there for me. You kept me from falling apart. You stayed on my team even when everyone else stopped believing in me. Just have to stay focus and follow my dreams. When I am on top of the world, I promise to let everyone know what you mean to me.

Someone

Once in a while, someone comes along that just takes you by surprise. Someone who just naturally brightens your day without notice. Someone who gives you a different perspective on life, including your own. Someone who simply makes each day feel so good, that just leaves you looking forward to the next. Someone so special like you.

Surprise

Listen to the sound of my voice, it is my disguise for your big surprise. Close your eyes, but don't worry because it's only a matter of time. Hold your head up high and turn your body to the side. Since you did everything right, please open your eyes because I am your big surprise.

Scared To Ask

Don't stop now. Don't even try to hid it. You don't have to say a word, but there is just something about you. I can't quite figure it out, yet my heart tells me otherwise. I don't know why, but I am dying inside to ask you. I better do it soon, no time to waste. Can't be scared, but what if you say…

Perfect

We are the perfect team. When I need you, you're always there for me. We can talk for hours about nothing, and I would do anything just to see you smile. You're so rare, sweet, and loving too. I never imagined meeting someone like you. We always lose track of time when we're together. Every second is a moment I wish would last forever. This day may pass us by, yet with you by my side, it just feels so right. Let me hold you and look into your eyes. You and me, the perfect two.

My Vows

Nunca podré separarme de tí. Nunca me iré de tú presencia. Nunca daré un paso adelante de tí, sabiendo que estas a mí lado. Nunca volveré a mirar atrás, porque Dios te puso en mí presente. Nunca pensé tomar tu mano, sin embargo, hasta tú corazón me diste.

Thinking Of

I've been thinking about flying away. I've been thinking about touching the night sky. I know I can do it, if I just believe it. I close my eyes as I start to let go. Nothing can hold me back, yet I feel my heart holding on for dear life. I can't take it anymore, it is time for me to...

Today Is The Day

A new day is like a blessing in disguise. I don't expect for nothing, but I'm just grateful to be alive. Just trying to beat the odds by no longer looking back. This is not just a one-time thing, but instead I am going to make it last. Always dreaming about a new day, but today is the day I been waiting for.

My Never Ending Book

If I could, for just one moment, write everything that is running through my mind, I would definitely write a never ending book. Some would read it and laugh like they never have before. Others may cry, and wonder if all of it was true. Very few would understand, but only one would know the meaning behind every page.

Others

Will I be known as a selfish person or will my good deeds make a difference? If I were to give it my all, would I be known as a fighter? If I were to stop and look at life, would I embrace it, or would I stand up for what is right? For if suffering is all that is left after I am gone, then remember me as compassion. Compassion by seeing beyond my own pain and instead attending to other's needs.

Willing To Be

If you could be anything in the world, would you be the greatest? Or would you be the hero everyone is waiting for? If you had to make a choice what would it be? Would you be willing to take a risk and just be the best? Or would you be the one who takes this world by surprise? Tell me, how are you ever going to know if you are not willing to be…

Who I Am

I am no hero, for I am always breaking all the rules. Gonna be the greatest because I just can't be second best. Can't wait for something, I'm instead working my way to the top from nothing. Looking back is not an option, going forward is all I know. It may take a lifetime, but this world will one day know who I am.

A Year Ago

A year has gone by and you are nowhere to be found. A year ago, you were standing by my side telling me how much you loved me. A year ago, I was having the time of my life because of you. I had no clue that a year later there would be nothing left between you and I. when I think of you, it kills me to know that you're no longer mine. A year has gone by, yet my love for you still remains the same. We may no longer be together, but I know someday things will be better, like a year ago.

Friends Forever

It almost seems like it was just yesterday that we were talking about today. We used to think things would never change, that our lives would just stay the same. But as time went by, we realized we were all moving on. Yet the memories will always remind us of all the good times we had. I will never say goodbye because as we go on, we will always be friends forever.

Smile, Laugh, And Hope

Smile, for it will go beyond the stars. Laugh, for joy is what fills our lungs. And Hope, for one day life will be different.

Yesterday Is A Thing Of The Past

Today is not just a moment, but a new beginning. Do not look at yesterday for you are blessed to no longer be there, but here. What you do with this new day is up to you. Don't waste another day in the past for you were taken from there and given today. Make this day count.

Thank You

I don't know if I've ever taken the time to thank you. But I should, because there's only one of you. You're the one who seems to know just how to find a rainbow behind every dark cloud. You know when to offer advice and when to just listen. You're so attuned to the feelings of others, that you're just a joy to be around with. I think it's time you knew how very much I appreciate you. How very glad I am to know you. So before I go on I just want to say, "Thank you!"

Learn

As time goes by, we start to realize that there is a difference. A difference beyond measure, which we will simply never understand. We learn that kisses are not contracts and presents will never be promises. We can finally see that company doesn't always mean security. That holding hands doesn't mean someone will stand by our side when we need them the most. In the end we begin to accept defeat with our head held high. We start to build roads on today, because tomorrow is too uncertain for plans. We learn, that after all we can endure, we really are strong. We really have worth. We learn our greatest lesson, which is that with every goodbye, we learn.

Notes

111

Lightning Source UK Ltd.
Milton Keynes UK
UKHW050902051220
374594UK00003B/102

9 781664 142336